*Saving Daylight*

# Books by Jim Harrison

POETRY

*Braided Creek: A Conversation in Poetry*, with Ted Kooser (Copper Canyon, 2003)
*The Shape of the Journey: New and Collected Poems* (Copper Canyon, 1998)
*After Ikkyū* (Shambhala, 1996)
*The Theory and Practice of Rivers and New Poems* (Clark City, 1989)
*Selected and New Poems: 1961–1981* (Delta/Seymour Lawrence, 1982)
*Returning to Earth* (Ithaca House, 1977)
*Letters to Yesenin* (Sumac, 1973)
*Outlyer and Ghazals* (Simon & Schuster, 1971)
*Locations* (W.W. Norton, 1968)
*Plain Song* (W.W. Norton, 1965)

NOVELS

*True North* (Grove Press, 2004)
*The Road Home* (Atlantic Monthly Press, 1998)
*Dalva* (E.P. Dutton/Seymour Lawrence, 1988)
*Sundog* (E.P. Dutton/Seymour Lawrence, 1984)
*Warlock* (Delacorte Press/Seymour Lawrence, 1981)
*Farmer* (Viking Press, 1976)
*A Good Day to Die* (Simon & Schuster, 1973)
*Wolf: A False Memoir* (Simon & Schuster, 1971)

NOVELLA TRILOGIES

*The Summer He Didn't Die* (Atlantic Monthly Press, 2005)
*The Beast God Forgot to Invent: Novellas* (Atlantic Monthly Press, 2000)
*Julip* (Houghton Mifflin/Seymour Lawrence, 1994)
*The Woman Lit by Fireflies* (Houghton Mifflin/Seymour Lawrence, 1990)
*Legends of the Fall* (Delacorte Press/Seymour Lawrence, 1979)

NONFICTION

*Off to the Side: A Memoir* (Atlantic Monthly Press, 2002)
*The Raw and the Cooked: Adventures of a Roving Gourmand* (Grove Press, 2001)
*Just Before Dark* (Clark City, 1991)

CHILDREN'S BOOKS

*The Boy Who Ran to the Woods* (Atlantic Monthly Press, 2000)

# JIM HARRISON

## SAVING DAYLIGHT

Copper Canyon Press

Copper Canyon Press gratefully acknowledges and thanks Russell Chatham for the use of his lithograph, *Moonrise Over the Roaring Fork River,* 22" × 26", 2004, and photographer Alec Soth for the use of his portrait of Jim Harrison, taken in Livingston, Montana, 2004.

Copper Canyon Press is in residence at Fort Worden State Park in Port Townsend, Washington, under the auspices of Centrum Foundation. Centrum is a gathering place for artists and creative thinkers from around the world, students of all ages and backgrounds, and audiences seeking extraordinary cultural enrichment.

LIBRARY OF CONGRESS CATALOGING-IN-PUBLICATION DATA

Harrison, Jim, 1937–
Saving daylight / by Jim Harrison.
  p.  cm.
ISBN 1-55659-235-3 (alk. paper)
ISBN 1-55659-242-6 (limited edition: alk. paper)
I. Title.
PS3558.A67S28 2006

2005028704

9 8 7 6 5 4 3 2   FIRST PRINTING

COPPER CANYON PRESS
Post Office Box 271
Port Townsend, Washington 98368

www.coppercanyonpress.org

*for Linda (again)*

ACKNOWLEDGMENTS

I must give thanks to William Barillas and María Ghiggia, who translated the four poems into Spanish.

Poems from *Saving Daylight* appeared in the following publications:

*American Life in Poetry:* "Marching"

*American Poetry Review:* "Modern Times," "Dream Love," "Becoming," "Hakuin and Welch"

*Border Beat:* "In Veracruz in 1941"

*Brick:* "Alcohol," "Time," "Letter Poem to Sam Hamill and Dan Gerber"

Copper Canyon Press broadsides: "Night Dharma," "Older Love"

*Dunes Review:* "A Letter to Ted & Dan"

*Exquisite Corpse:* "Young Love," "After the War"

*Five Points:* "Reading Calasso," "The Bear," "To a Meadowlark," "November," "Joseph's Poem"

*Good Poems for Hard Times,* Garrison Keillor, ed. (New York: Viking): "Easter Morning"

*Men's Journal:* "Bars"

*The Midwest Quarterly:* "An Old Man," "Brothers and Sisters"

*New Letters:* "Cabbage," "Angry Women," "Alcohol," "Two Girls," "On the Way to the Doctor's," "L'envoi"

*New York Times Book Review:* "The Old Days"

*Open City:* "Adding It Up," "Easter Morning," "Saving Daylight"

*Poets Against the War:* "Poem of War (i)" and "Poem of War (ii)" appeared as a single poem, "Poem of War"

Pressed Wafer Broadsides for John Wieners: "Portal, Arizona"

*TriQuarterly:* "Effluvia," "Memorial Day"

*The Writer's Almanac:* "Older Love," "Easter Morning"

"Livingston Suite" first appeared as a letterpress chapbook from Limberlost Press

# Contents

*Saving Daylight*

# Water

Before I was born I was water.
I thought of this sitting on a blue
chair surrounded by pink, red, white
hollyhocks in the yard in front
of my green studio. There are conclusions
to be drawn but I can't do it anymore.
Born man, child man, singing man,
dancing man, loving man, old man,
dying man. This is a round river
and we are her fish who become water.

# Cabbage

If only I had the genius of a cabbage
or even an onion to grow myself
in their laminae from the holy core
that bespeaks the final shape. Nothing
is outside of us in this overinterpreted world.
Bruises are the mouths of our perceptions.
The gods who have died are able to come
to life again. It's their secret that they wish
to share if anyone knows that they exist.
Belief is a mood that weighs nothing on anyone's
scale but nevertheless exists. The moose
down the road wears the black cloak of a god
and the dead bird lifts from a bed of moss
in a shape totally unknown to us.
It's after midnight in Montana.
I test the thickness of the universe, its resilience
to carry us further than any of us wish to go.
We shed our shapes slowly like moving water,
which ends up as it will so utterly far from home.

## Mom and Dad

Gentle readers, feel your naked belly button where
you were tied to your mother. Kneel and thank
her for your jubilant but woebegone life. Don't
for a moment think of the mood of your parents
when you were conceived which so vitally affects
your destiny. You have no control over that and
it's unprofitable to wonder if they were pissed
off or drunk, bored, watching television news,
listening to country music, or hopefully out in
the orchard grass feeling the crunch of wind-
fall apples under their frantic bodies.

# Night Dharma

How restlessly the Buddha sleeps
between my ears, dreaming his dreams
of emptiness, writing his verbless poems.
(I almost rejected "green tree
white goat red sun blue sea.")
Verbs are time's illusion, he says.

In the stillness that surrounds us
we think we have to probe our wounds,
but with what? Mind caresses mind
not by saying *no* or *yes* but *neither.*

Turn your watch back to your birth
for a moment, then way ahead beyond
any expectation. There never was a coffin
worth a dime. These words emerge
from the skin as the sweat of gods
who drink only from the Great Mother's breasts.

Buddha sleeps on, disturbed when I disturb
him from his liquid dreams of blood and bone.
Without comment he sees the raven carrying
off the infant snake, the lovers' foggy
gasps, the lion's tongue that skins us.

One day we dozed against a white pine stump
in a world of dogwood and sugar plum blossoms.
An eye for an eye, he said, trading
a left for my right, the air green tea
in the sky's blue cup.

# Modern Times

### I

Each man should own three
belts just as he once had three
legs the better to turn corners.
Women had three arms
the better to hold things.
Now without these extra limbs
men and women can't remember
the life they don't know they've forgotten
packed away with dried plum buds
and evening primroses. They've traded
their limbs for clocks and ideas,
their hearts packed in salt. They thought
it was noon but it's nearly midnight.

### II

Every poem is the poem
before the last. We know this absurd
feeling of wishing to live on the lip
of a future that can't quite
manage to happen, the ache
of the girl who decided not to exist
before she was born, the quizzical
trashcan behind the abortion clinic,
the unacknowledged caskets that always
arrive on night flights. We assumed
God loved most the piety of beggars,
that we should properly cower before
our elected murderers, that we could

sit tight behind our locked doors
and try to pretend we were rich
and happy children until time wore out.

III

We worked for food and shelter
and then bought the arts and better cars,
bigger houses, smarter children
who couldn't really learn to read and write.
It was too hard. The arts escaped
to a different heaven to get rid of us.
We misunderstood food and shelter,
flies crawling on a window,
fluttering up and down,
seeing the outside beyond reach
because of the invention of glass
that couldn't be undone. We lived
within the outside for two million years
and now it's mostly photos.
We chose wallpaper and paint over leaves
and rivers. In our dream of safety
we decided not to know the world.

IV

The question is, does the dog
remember her childhood?
If so, our universe changes,
tilts a bit. We do not willingly
offer much to the creature world,
a little food to amuse our loneliness.
We made funeral pyres of the houses
of bears and birds because they neglected
to console our paths to fortune.
They commit love with an intensity

unknown to us and without advice.
They read the world rather than books
and don't bother with names to identify
themselves. To them we're a Chinese film
without subtitles. Meanwhile my dog
dreams back to her seven-week childhood
in Wisconsin, over so soon before she took
a flight west to Montana, emerging
from a crate with a quizzical smile.

V

Do more people die asleep or awake?
We can easily avoid both conditions
but I'm not telling you how.
Why interrupt the ancient flow?
There's nothing more solid in life
than the will toward greed and self-destruction
but also beauty, who doesn't mind
sitting on her own tired knees.
How can I find my mother and father,
a sister and a brother if they're dead?
I've had to learn other languages
to make contact, the creature world
and flora, the mute landscape
offering a quiet music without verbs
and nouns. This is the language
of the departed ones. Those who have become
birds seem happy to be no longer us.
Salvation isn't coming. It's always been here.

VI

I've been on a full-time moon
watch this winter for reasons
I can't determine. Maybe I'm helping out?

My government is so loathsome I've turned
to other, much more important things.
The beetle takes a half hour on a leisurely
stroll across the patio, heading
northwest as if it truly mattered.
I think of Wallace Stevens in his office
doing insurance work as if it truly mattered.
He stays late on a spring afternoon
watching swallows swoop for insects
that haven't yet hatched in Hartford,
an old poet greedy for the life
he was never remotely to have;
a white marriage, love as a cold
cinderblock never to arise from the rubble,
his life a long slow Dresden
burning its own jealous ashes.

VII

I can freely tie myself up without rope.
This talent is in the realm of antimagic
and many people have it. On a dawn
walk despite the creek, birds and forest
I have to get through the used part,
the murky fluid of rehearsals
and resentments, but then they drain away
and I'm finally where I already am,
smack-dab in the middle of each step,
the air you can taste, the evening
primrose that startled by my visit
doesn't turn away. When I read
the ancient manuscripts of earth
many of the lines are missing
that I'm expected to complete.
I'm the earth, too, sharing this song

of blood and bone with the whale,
monkey and house cat. At eye level
with toad our eyes share the passage
of this ghost ship we boarded at birth.

VIII

There are a lot of muted grays in life,
dull bronzes, mornings the color
of a lead sinker that will never help
you catch a fish, and then a trace
of sun allows you to see down into the water
where three minnows pass diagonally above
a sunken log, two tadpoles, the pebble-
circular swirl of a spawning bed, a glutinous
clot of frog eggs, and farther out
a turtle peering above a lily pad's edge.
Salvation from mood can be slow
in coming. Two song sparrows pick
this moment to fight over a lady,
a private woodland Iraq shrieking
"She's mine," as she pretends to be otherwise
occupied. The sky doesn't study
our immobility. When the mood has fled
I listen to the air, and a cloud is only
a cloud again though I'd like to see a dragon
emerging upward to the water's surface,
a gesture to lift us above our human weight.

IX

I salute the tiny insect crawling
back and forth across my journal,
perhaps eating the infinitesimal particles
of dried sweat from the effort to make music
and reason out of the ocean of life

most often opaque as dirty cream.
I tell this insect how unlucky for him.
He should be outside eating the tender cores
of spring flowers or alighting on a bird's
back the better to fly away on another's wings.
Our lives are novels we don't want to read
and we so gracelessly translate their world
for our own purposes. We live morosely
in this graveyard long before we're buried.
Still we love our green and blue world
and leap out of our lives from sea to shining
sea. We know that our despised world
is our Great Mother's breast warm to our desert lips.


      x

What I'm doing is what I'm already
doing. The mind can't accept the ordinary.
The pope fed through his nose would prefer
pasta marinara as he grabs at heaven
as a gentle old monkey might at a vine
while hanging from a tree because of the waiting
jaguar far below. Finding myself where I already
am is a daily chore. Chaos herself is fragile.
A step takes seconds. Clocks leak our invisible
blood in invisible increments. I'd rather say,
"sun is up, high brutal noon, sun is down,
night comes," in rhythm with the bird's superior
clock. I can no longer reshape the unbearable
world and have given up to count birds.
Up the mountain in a mesquite thicket
two pale-blue female lazuli buntings yield
to the tally clicker in my vest pocket,
their souls intact, ignoring my glorious smile.
I've abandoned the culture's ghost not my life,
Jim on the south slope at dawn counting birds.

# Adding It Up

I forgot long division but does one
go into sixty-six more than sixty-six times?
There's the mother, two daughters, eight dogs,
I can't name all the cats and horses, a farm
for thirty-five years, then Montana, a cabin,
a border casita, two grandsons, two sons-in-law,
and graced by the sun and the moon, red wine
and garlic, lakes and rivers, the millions of trees.
I can't help but count out of habit, the secret
door underneath the vast stump where I founded
the usual Cro-Magnon religion, a door
enveloped by immense roots through which one day
I watched the passing legs of sandhill cranes,
napping where countless bears have napped,
an aperture above where the sky and the gods
may enter, yet I'm without the courage to watch
the full moon through this space. I can't figure
out a life. We're groundlings who wish to fly.
I live strongly in the memories of my dead dogs.
It's just a feeling that memories float around
waiting to be caught. I miss the cat that perched
on my head during zazen. Since my brother died
I've claimed the privilege of speaking to local rocks,
trees, birds, the creek. Last night a broad moonbeam
fell across my not-so-sunken chest. The smallest
gods ask me what there is beyond consciousness,
the moment by moment enclosure the mind
builds to capture the rudiments of time.
Two nights ago I heard a woman from across
the creek, a voice I hadn't heard since childhood.

I didn't answer. Red was red this dawn
after a night of the swirling milk of stars
that came too close. I felt lucky not to die.
My brother died at high noon one day in Arkansas.
Divide your death by your life and you get
a circle, though I'm not so good at math.
This morning I sat in the dirt playing
with five cow dogs, giving out a full pail of biscuits.

## Young Love

In my "Memoir of an Unsuccessful Prostitute"
I questioned what was it like to be nineteen
in New York City in 1957, fresh from northern
Michigan farmland, looking for sex and food.
First of all the edges of buildings were sharp
and if you walked around a corner too close
to them you could cut yourself. Even though it
was summer the daylight was short and when it
was hot you sweated inward. You walked the streets
as a shy elephant who within the cruelty
of his neurons had conceived a love of women.
A black woman said you were too white
and a white woman said you were too brown.
Another said you were a red Indian ("How
exciting"). You became very thin and fell asleep
beside fountains, on park benches, in the library
where they roused you with a shake. Pigeons
avoided you as a breadless monster. The circus women
paid in used popcorn, their secret currency.
The beatnik girl paid with crabs who tugged
at the roots of your eyebrows, your tiny friends.
Late one night the moon split in pieces
and you could see two yellow shards at the ends
of Forty-second Street where a herring sandwich
was a quarter, Italian sausage fifty cents.
The drug of choice was a Benzedrine inhaler
plus three beers, after which you jumped over the hood
of an approaching taxi with your invisible pogo stick.
You hitchhiked the trail of a letter from a girl back home
and New York City became more beautiful
with each mile west.

# The Movie

I'm making a movie about my life
which never ends. The plot thickens
and thickens like an overcooked soup.
The movie features tens of thousands
of characters including those who passed
me on the street without knowing
that I was a star. The film includes
my long horizontal dives above fields
of corpses. I've become proud that I'm part
dog favoring perceptions over conclusions.
I'm not sexy enough at my age
to carry a movie so I'm filming my mind
at play, with the rudiments of Eros
backing into the camera with the force
of a drop forge. Ultimately the poet, filmmaker,
is the girl who didn't have a date for the prom.
She takes a walk and hears the music
from the gymnasium, imagining the crepe
paper and wilting corsages vibrating
with the wretched music. She walks past
the graveyard with its heavy weight
of dirt nappers and climbs a hill steep
as a cow's face. From the top of the hill
she sees the world she never made
but has changed with words into the arena
of the sacred. The sky becomes
dumbfounded with her presence. If she decides
to shoot herself it's only to come to life again.
The thin slip of the moon speaks French
but the voice is compressed by trees and translated

by fireflies. This girl is far more interesting
than I am and that's why I'm filming
her rather than my trip to the mailbox
avoiding the usual rattlesnakes in the tallgrass.
It's not truth that keeps us alive
but invention, no actual past but the stories
we've devised to cover our disappearing
asses. Near a pond she hears the millions of
tree frogs, peepers, and thinks this noise is sex.
For a split second she wonders what it would
be like to make love to that older poet she heard
read in Grand Rapids, the way he grasped
her hand when he gave her a free book. My god,
now we're nearly together in my movie though
the camera is the unwilling POV and when it
comes CLOSE she pushes down her jeans
near the thicket where I've been waiting.
In the faintest moonlight I see her pelvic curls.
Now it is time to back away from heaven's mouth.
I don't film dreams that lack narrative drive,
and besides I have no legs to leave the thicket,
only an imagination whose camera has chosen
to BACK AWAY far above the crucified dogs
and the soldiers writhing in alien courtyards,
above the swirling cumuli where those who we
thought were dead watch us while sitting on plastic
lounge chairs, up where the finest music still rises,
up there out of harm's way where I store my life film
in microversion around the neck of a hawk who has
never landed since birth.

# Livingston Suite

*in memory of T.J. Huth*

Shorn of nature,
here but in small supply,
townspeople adore their dogs.

•◆•

Our dogs have never lived
in a town. Neither have I
since 1967. I adore
the puzzlement of our dogs.

•◆•

Each morning I walk four blocks
to this immense river,
surprised that it's still there,
that it won't simply disappear
into the ground like the rest of us.

•◆•

In the burnt July air
the strange cool odor
of sprinkler water
creating its own little breeze
in the Livingston Park
where there are twelve rings for playing
horseshoes built before the fathers of lies
built the clouds above our heads.

·◆·

A lovely girl passes on her bicycle
with a fat cat
on her shoulder who watches me
disappear through heavy lids,
then a lovely soiled girl on her knees
in a garden looks up at me
to say hello. A Christian urge tries
to make me ignore her pretty butt
cocked upward like a she-cat's.


·◆·


Four churches within a block,
Methodist, Lutheran, Episcopal, Congregational,
surrounding me with maudlin holiness,
Sunday's hymns a droning hum
against the ceilings. Crows and magpies think,
Oh it's that day again.
Christ in the New World like Milne's Eeyore,
a lumpen donkey sweating with our greed,
trying to make us shepherd his billions of birds.


·◆·


Under the streets are the remnants
of an older town with caches
of Indian skulls, also wizened
white scalps from those who jumped
the gun on the westward movement
that is still ending in Santa Monica
where a girl I knew who, after taking three
California speedballs, had her brain hurled into eternity
like a jellied softball. Oh Cynthia.

·◆·

I walk my dog Rose in the alleys
throughout town. Maybe it's where poets belong,
these substreets where the contents of human life
can be seen more clearly, our shabby backsides
disappearing into the future at the precise rate
of the moon's phases. Rose turns, hearing
an upstairs toilet flush, the dead cows,
pigs and chickens turning semiliquid
in the guts of strangers, the pretty tomato
changing shape, the potatoes that once held leaves
and blossoms in their spindly green arms. Holy days
of early summer with lilacs drooping laden
under the weight of their moist art. From a kitchen
a woman laughs a barking laugh over
something I'll never know. A ninety-year-old
couple emerges from the Methodist church smiling,
masters of a superior secret. Back in the alley
a dirty yellow cat emerges from a garbage can
with trout remains, a sure sign of feline victory.
She holds the carcass tightly as if I might take it.


·◆·


Our newspaper, *The Enterprise,* said,
"Grizzlies feasting on storm-killed cattle."
An early June blizzard dropped four feet
of snow, killing a thousand cows and calves,
a few foals, and the grizzlies hungry and fresh
from hibernation are feasting. "The bears
are just thick. It's really kind of dangerous
up here right now," said Gus V., a rancher.
Interesting news on the summer solstice.

The cow protrudes from the snowbank with ravens
perched around the eyes & udders watching for a coyote
or bear to open the hidebound meat, nearly
a million pounds of meat spread around the
countryside. What pleasure in this natural terrorism.

·◆·

On a twilight walk a violent storm moved swiftly
toward the east and south of me with the starkest
lightning striking against the slate-colored
Absaroka mountains. Closer, on a green mountainside
white trucks passed on Interstate 90,
then closer yet Watson's Black Angus cattle
sprinkled like peppercorns against shiny
wet pale green grass. Closer, a tormented
cottonwood thicket in the rising wind, maybe
60 knots, branches flailing, closer the broad
and turbulent brown river. And finally
only me on which all things depend, standing
on the riverbank, bent to the wind, the solitary
twilight watcher wondering who is
keeping the gods alive this evening or whether
they have given up on us and our tiny forked tongues,
our bleating fears and greed, our pastel anxieties.

·◆·

In 1968 when I was first here
there was a cool scent of pines
and melting snow from the mountains
carried by a southwind through the river's
canyon. The scent is still here,
the sure fresh odor of the West.

At the oars of the drift boat
in the thrash and churn of a rapid
I have no more control over the boat,
or my life, than I had in 1968.
Swept away. And not quite understanding
that this water is heading toward
the Caribbean. A grizzly bear pisses
in a creek in the Absarokas and traces end up
nonchalantly passing New Orleans
into the Gulf of Mexico. This fuzzy air
above is from dust storms in China.
The underground river far below me
started in the Arctic and heads toward
the equator. During the Bush colonoscopy
narwhals were jousting over lady narwhals
and an immense Venezuelan anaconda gave birth
to a hundred miniatures of her kind, all quickly
eaten by waiting caimans and large wading birds.
Trapped in the compartment of a sunken ship
a man writes a letter in the dark to his wife
and children in Missouri which will never be read.
I watch a blind sheep who loves to roll in the grass.


•◆•


At the rodeo the bucking horse
leaps then buckles to its knees,
recovers, then bucks up. And up.
The rider thrown, eating a face-
ful of dirt while behind the announcer's
shack and across the river,
up a cliff and a broad green slope,

trucks pass east and west on I-90
unmindful of the cowboy spitting dirt.

　　•◆•

Around here they're still voting
for Eisenhower as a write-in candidate.
Around here people still have memories
and honor their war dead. In the park
to each road guardrail a flag and white cross
are attached, and a name that is gone
but not forgotten. An old man carrying
a portable oxygen unit breathes deeply
with moist eyes looking at his brother's name,
lost in Iwo Jima. We bow slightly
to each other, and my memory repeats the prayer
I offered at age five for my uncles Art and Walter
off in the South Pacific on warships fighting
the Japanese and the satanic Tojo. At church
we sang "Fairest Lord Jesus" and the minister
announced that a deacon's son was lost
in what I heard as "yurp."
Some of the men and women sobbed loudly.
I remembered him playing baseball and driving
around town in his old Ford coupe with an actual
squirrel tail attached to the aerial, and just out
of kindergarten I had it all wrong thinking who will
drive Fred's car now? Our mothers and fathers embraced.

　　•◆•

From different upstairs windows I see four different
mountain ranges not there to accompany the four churches:
the Absarokas, the Gallatins, the Bridgers, the Crazies.

You naturally love a mountain range called Crazies.
Of course naked women, Native and white,
run through the Crazies on moonlit nights
howling for husbands and lovers
lost to our wars. I've followed their red footprints
while hunting in these mountains, the small toes.

·◆·

A community can drown in itself,
then come to life again. Every yard seems
to have flowers, every street its resident magpies.
In the outfield of the baseball diamond
there are lovely small white flowers that a gardener
told me are the "insidious bindweed." All my life
I've liked weeds. Weeds are botanical
poets, largely unwanted. You can't make a dollar
off them. People destroy the obnoxious dandelion
that I've considered a beautiful flower since early
childhood, blowing off the fuzzy seeds when they died,
sending the babies off into the grim universe,
but then I'm also fond of cowbirds and crows,
cowbirds and poets laying their eggs for others
to raise then drifting away for no reason.

·◆·

Search & Rescue is "combing" the river
this morning for a drowned boy. If it were me
I'd rather float east through the night toward the rising
sun. But it's not me. The boy probably
wasn't literary and the parents want the body
to bury, the fourth body in the river this summer.
Currents can hold a body tight to the bottom.

A vet friend found residual gills in the head
of a dog but at our best we're ungainly in water
compared to the clumsiest of fishes. Against the song,
we won't fly away. Or float. We sink into earth.

     •◆•

In this prolonged heat wave the snow
is shrinking upward to the mountain tip-tops
to a few crevasses and ravines. On Mount Wallace
ancient peoples, likely the Crow, the Absarokas,
carved out of flat stone the imprint of a man
so you could lie there in a grizzly-claw necklace
and see only sky for three days and nights,
a very long session in your own private church.

     •◆•

It's ninety-five degrees at four PM
and two girls in their early teens step
from the cooler cement sidewalk onto the street's hot
asphalt in their bare feet, beginning to dance,
jump, prance, one in shorts and the other
in a short summer dress. It is good enough
so that only Mozart would contribute to this pure
dance that is simply what it is, beyond passing
lust, sheer physical beauty, the grace of *being*
on a nearly insufferable hot day in Montana.
The girls skidded their feet on sprinkler-wet grass
under a maple tree, then went indoors out of my life.

Everyone seems to have loved the drowned boy.
Destiny is unacceptable. This grand river
he'd seen thousands of times didn't wait for him.

Nobody seems to have a clue. He died two days ago
and they're still searching the river. Some men
carry ominous long poles with a hook in the end.
This morning walking Rose I looked at the wide
eddy with a slow but inexorable whirlpool coiling
in upon itself that no human could swim against.
You might survive by giving up the struggle
and hope that the water would cast you aside
into the steady current, and that it wouldn't force you
downward beyond the limit of your breath.
In high school I flunked chemistry, unable to bear
up under the foreign odors or comprehend the structure
of water. It's one thing to say out loud "H-two-O,"
and another to have spent thousands of days in the company
of lakes, creeks and rivers seeing fish breathe
this liquid air. An old man feels the slow struggle
of dying, say for ten years, which drowning shortens
to a minute or so. People say it's the best way to die.
Once in the Humboldt current off the coast of Ecuador
I looked into the eye of a whale and later wondered
if she communed with the soul of water. At nineteen
or twenty the cup is overflowing but not understood.
The dread is there won't be time to drink it.

Kooser called from Nebraska to say he'd found
a large cinder on a long walk along abandoned
country railroad tracks, a remnant of steam

trains, the cinder similar to those our fathers
shoveled from coal furnaces in the early winter mornings
before stoking the fire. In your dark bedroom
you'd hear the scrape of the shovel and the thump
when cinders were dropped in metal washtubs.
Now the trains are all diesel and in Livingston at night
I hear them pass, Burlington & Northern, the horn
an immense bassoon warning the drunks at crossings.
Some complain but I love this night music,
imagining that a few of the railroad cars are from
my youth when I stood in a pasture and thrilled
to my favorite, "Route of Phoebe Snow."
To be excited by a cinder is to be excited about life.

·◆·

There's a dullish ache, a restlessness in those
who walk their dogs along the river's levee.
None of us wants to find the body
but then it's our duty to look in this early morning
light with a cool breeze coming off the crumpled water.
A tree plucked from the bank sails by and beauty
is visited by the terror of power. When my sister
was killed at nineteen I began to disbelieve
in destiny, in clocks and calendars, that the downward
thrust of time that hammers us into the ground
is planned, that the girl in France who wrote
me a letter before suicide was drawn to that place
by an ignored, thus insignificant, universe where God
wakes up cross, yawns and the dead are tossed
like confetti into the void. If there's a divinity
that shapes our ends it's beyond our ken. A tree
by its nature seeks its future moment by moment.
The child in grade-school science looks out the window

bemused that his singularity was chosen from millions
of his parents' eggs and sperms. There's much less time
than he thinks no matter how long he lives. The heart
can never grasp these unbearable early departures.

• ◆ •

A concert in the park on the 4th of July sponsored
by the networks in New York. Someone named Sheryl Crow,
Hank Williams Junior not Senior, and my old favorite,
Los Lobos. As a claustrophobe I can't walk the four blocks
into the crowds but from my studio
I can hear the Latino music wafting through maple
trees, imagining I'm at our winter casita near Patagonia,
Arizona, on the Mexican border, the music so much
closer to love and death than our own, the heart
worn on the sleeve, the natural lament of flowers, the moon
visible. Smiling skeletons are allowed to dance
and the gods draw closer to earth, the cash registers
drowned out in the flight of birds, the sound of water.

• ◆ •

You can't row or swim upstream on the river.
This moving water is your continuing past
that you can't retrace by the same path
that you reached the present, the moment by moment
implacable indifference of time. At one point
in my life nearly every tree on earth was shorter
than me, and none of the birds presently here
were here at my birth except an aged macaw
in Bahia. Not a single bear or bug, dog or cat,
but a few turtles and elephants who greeted
my arrival. We can't return for a second

to those golden days of the Great Depression, World War II,
the slaughter of the Jews, the Stalinist purges,
the yellow horde of China feeding on its afterbirth,
the Japanese gearing up scientific experiments
that would kill a quarter of a million. How auspicious
it is when people talk of the marvelous sixties
with the extermination of JFK, Bobby Kennedy,
Martin Luther King, Vietnam, and enough music
to divert us from the blood-splattered screen
of immediate history. Within time and the river
no one catches their breath, a vast prayer wheel
without a pivot spinning off into the void.
We're wingless birds perpetually falling north.

                    ·—·

Maybe I'm wrong. After years of practice
I learned to see as a bird but I refuse
to do it now, not wanting to find the body.
I traveled east to our cabin in Michigan
where I learned that my Zen master, Kobun
Chino Sensei, drowned in a cold pond trying to save
his three-year-old daughter, who also drowned.
I make nothing of this but my mind suddenly
rises far upward and I see Kobun in his black
robes struggling in the water and he becomes
a drowning raven who then frees himself for flight,
his daughter on the pond's bottom rising to join him.
What could the vision mean but a gift? I said
maybe I'm wrong. The Resurrection is fatally correct.

As an early and relentless swimmer I couldn't imagine
death by water until I saw a spring runoff
in the Manistee River, a shed floating by
as if powered by a motor, a deafening wave curling
upward at a log jam. I don't want to die
in a car, at war, in an airliner where I searched
for the pulse of an old lady who collapsed
in the aisle, found nothing, and everyone said
she seemed to be smiling. She left the plane behind.
But water at least is an earthly embrace.
It was my wife who found the body while walking
her dog Mary beside the river at Mayor's landing.
I was in Michigan in a cabin beside the river
made turbulent by an hour-long cloudburst.
I wish it wasn't you, I said. "But it was," she said.
"It had to be someone. Why not me?"


•❖•


In Livingston I'm back home in Reed City
over fifty years ago when trains were steam but the cows
and alleys were the same, the friendly town mongrels
I said hello to, one who walked with me an hour
before turning home when we crossed his street.
From the park bridge I watch a heron feed and at the edge
of town there were yellow legs, Wilson's phalaropes
wandering a sand and rock bar, at home in the river
because they could fly over it. I'm going to swim
across it on a moonlit night. Near the porch steps
of the house next door are two stone Chinese lions
looking at the street with the eyes of small gods,
the eyes that were given us that we don't wish to use

for fear of madness. Beside the river's bend
where he drowned colored stones are arranged
to say "We love you, T.J." Not loved in past
tense but love in the way that the young have the grace
of their improbable affections, their hearts
rising to the unkempt breath and beat of the earth.

# Hill

For the first time
far in the distance
he could see his twilight,
wrapping around the green hill
where three rivers start,
and sliding down toward him
through the trees until it reached
the blueberry marsh and stopped,
telling him to go away, not now,
not for the time being.

# Buried Time

Our bodies leap ahead
and behind our years.

Our bodies tracked the sun
with numbers at play and curiosity
not for slavery.

Time often moves sideways,
its mouth full and choking
on rubbery clocks.

In the elephant's heart
the uncounted sunrises, the muscle
pumping blood to its
red music.

The world's air is full
of orphaned ghosts and on the ground
so many mammals that feed
at night for safety.

Our bodies move sideways
and backwards of their own accord
in scorn of time.

I didn't divorce the sun and moon
but we had an amicable separation
for a while.

I established myself in the night.
I organized seven nights in a row
without any days.

I liked best the slender cracks
between nights and days where I bloomed
like an apple tree.

I collected dawns and twilights.
They are stored in my room between
two volumes of poetry, their titles secret.

In geologic time we barely exist.
I collected memories of my temporary host
leaving a trace of words, my simian tracks.

The universe is the Great Mother.
I haven't met the father. My doubt
is the patina of shit the culture
paints on my psyche.

There is no "I" with the sun and moon.
Time means only the irretrievable.
If I mourn myself, the beloved dead,
I must mourn the deaths of galaxies.

Despite gravity we're fragile as shadows.
They crushed us with time-as-money,
the linear hoax.

At the cabin standing in the river
on a warm night the female coyote
near the logjam can see the moon's glint
off my single front tooth.

When she barks her voice wraps
itself with me in the moving water,
the holy form of time.

## Angry Women

Women in peignoirs are floating around
the landscape well out of eyesight
let alone reach. They are as palpable
as the ghost of my dog Rose whom I see
on long walks, especially when exhausted
and my half-blind eyes are blurred by cold wind
or sleet or snow. The women we've mistreated
never forgive us nor should they, thus their ghostly
energies thrive at dawn and twilight in this vast
country where any of the mind's movies can be played
against this rumpled wide-screened landscape.
Our souls are travelers. You can tell when your own
is gone, and then these bleak, improbable
visits from others, their dry tears because you were
never what you weren't, so that the world
becomes only what it is, the unforgiving flow
of an unfathomable river. Still they wanted you otherwise,
closer to their dreamchild, just as you imagined
fair maidens tight to you as decals to guide
you toward certainties. The new pup, uncrippled by ideals,
leaps against the fence, leaps at the mountains beyond.

## Before the Trip

When old people travel, it's for relief
from a life that they know too well,
not routine but the very long slope
of disbelief in routine, the unbearable
lightness of brushing teeth that aren't all
there, the weakened voice calling out
for the waiter who doesn't turn;
the drink that once was neither here
nor there is now a singular act of worship.
The sun that rises every day says
*I don't care* to the torments of love
and hate that once pushed one back
and forth on the blood's red wagon.
All dogs have become beautiful
in the way they look at cats and wonder
what to do. Breakfast is an event
and bird flu only a joke of fear the world
keeps playing. On the morning walk
the horizon is ours when we wish.
We know that death is a miracle for everyone
or so the gods say in a whisper of rain
in the immense garden we couldn't quite trace.

## Paris Television

Thinking of those Russian schoolchildren. How can what we call depression be approached directly? It can't. I have this triumverate of ghosts – John, Rose, Suzanne Wilson – who visit me. Mortality is gravity, the weight we bear up under daily. I can only create lightness out of doors – walking, fishing, standing in the yard looking at Linda's flowers or the Absaroka mountains, or in the Upper Peninsula looking at the peculiar vastness of Lake Superior, the night sky, watching my grandsons. How can I lift my weight each day when my own words began to fail me this year, or my perceptions began to fail my words? When both my inside and outside worlds became incomprehensible? But then the source of all religion is incomprehension. The first day of school for the Russian children. Their dogs walk halfway, figure it out, return home to wait in the just-beginning-to-wane summer heat, with all flowers shedding themselves and neglected wheat stalks in the corners of fields dropping their grains, some dogs howling at the fireworks, and then the parents of the children joining them. My voice becomes small as a molting bird's, barely a whisper until I can fly again, if ever.

# Opal

O Opal, your ear
in my heart
both hear
the glorious void,
preferring the birds.

# The Man Who Looked for Sunlight

Nine days of dark, cold rain
in October, some snow, three gales
off Lake Superior with the cabin's tin roof
humming Beethoven, the woodcock weather vane
whirling and thumping like a kettledrum,
tree limbs crashing in the woods;
at dawn a gust made small whitecaps on the river.
Marquette NPR promised sunlight
on Thursday. I sit here reflecting
I've burned a whole cord of wood this week.
I'm ten years old again sitting here waiting
for the sunlight, petting my dog Rose,
sitting by the window straining for sunlight.
I'm not going to drown myself in the cold
dark river but I really would like sunlight.
Finally clouds rush by well beyond the speed
limit, and there's a glimpse of sunlight,
a few seconds of sunlight, enough for today,
the sunlight glistening on the wet forest
and my dog sleeping by the window.

# Alcohol

In the far back room of the school
for young writers are two big illegal
formaldehyde glass jars holding the kidneys
and livers of Faulkner and Hemingway
among the tens of thousands of empty bottles
of everything they drank to fuel themselves
through their bloody voyages. Alive, their arms
were crooked out as question marks trying
to encircle the world. Dead, they are crazy
old men who convinced us of the reasonableness
of their tales, their books deducted from their caskets
at the last possible moment. And now we hold
them tightly as if they ever truly cared.
No one should wish to enter this room
but still some of us hurl ourselves against
the invisible door as if our stories and alcohol
were Siamese twins ineluctably joined at the head,
our hearts enlarged until they can barely beat.

# En Veracruz en 1941

Giselle me dio una estatuilla primitiva
de la Virgen de Sonora, estrellas radiando de su cabeza,
labios y cejas astillados, nariz descascarada
y debajo de su manto el niño
Jesús mira saludando con dos manos
elevadas, anunciando su llegada entre nosotros.
Giselle, ningún hombre puede acostarse con las tres:
madre, amante, Virgen.
Confieso que tus pezones son rojo rubí
pero en la muerte se tornarán turquesas.
Con tu pie desnudo sobre mi falda confieso también
que me despojaré de tu insoportable estatuilla,
o camino a La Habana la dejaré caer en el océano,
para que descanse en la falda del poeta de América, Hart Crane,
quien no pudo aprender el lenguaje de los chiles y las flores,
que la mar es madre no padre. No podemos estar solos.
¿Dónde estaba el perro para acariciar la mano con la que escribía?
Perro, te doy mi segunda empanada,
la sonrisa roja de mi corazón, el crepúsculo que lleva la mar
a mi cuarto donde Giselle duerme bien desnuda
sobre su vientre para que yo aúlle sin voz
al Caribe, porque no soy un perro de buena fe,
soy un perro poético a quien la luna devuelve con un aullido
su mensaje espantoso de llegada y despedida.
Madre, Virgen, amante sobre su vientre. Las tres son una,
pero estamos en partes, pies y cabeza de alguna manera
arrastrándose hacia nuestros cuerpos, moviéndose como yo ahora
bajo el ventilador, meciéndonos perpetuamente. Madre, Virgen,
perdónennos nuestras amantes. Una vez ustedes fueron mujeres.

~ *probablemente escrito por Pablo Neruda*

## In Veracruz in 1941

Giselle gave me a primitive statuette
of the Virgin from Sonora, stars spoked from her head,
chipped lips and eyebrows, flaked nose,
and from underneath her skirt the infant
Jesus peeks out saluting with two raised
hands, announcing his arrival among us.
Giselle, no man can sleep with all three:
mother, lover, Virgin.
I confess that your nipples are ruby
but at death they will become turquoise.
With your bare foot in my lap I also confess
I'll leave your unbearable statuette behind,
or en route to Havana drop it in the ocean,
to rest in the lap of America's poet, Hart Crane,
who could not learn the language of chilies and flowers,
that the sea is mother not father. We can't be alone.
Where was the dog to caress his writing hand?
Dog, I give you my second empanada,
my heart's red smile, the twilight that carries the sea
into my room where Giselle sleeps quite naked
on her belly so that I give a voiceless howl
to the Caribbean, not being a bona fide dog
but a poetic dog at whom the moon howls back
her terrifying message of arriving and leave-taking.
Mother, Virgin, lover on her belly. The three are one,
but we are in parts, feet and head somehow
crawling toward our bodies, moving as I do now
under the fan endlessly rocking, Mother, Virgin,
forgive us our lovers. You were women once.

                    ~ *very likely by Pablo Neruda (translated by Jim Harrison)*

## Dream Love

How exhausted we can become
from the contents of dreams:
long, too long nights of love
with whirling corrupted faces,
unwilling visits from the dead
whom we never quite summoned;
the animals who chased our souls
at noon when we were children
so that we wished to be magical dogs
running backwards off the world's
edge into a far better place
than a hot noon with earth herself
a lump in our weary young throats.
In dream love we're playing
music to an empty room.
On leaving the room the music
continues and surrounds those we loved
and lost who are at roost
in their forested cemeteries,
visible but forever beyond our reach.
They won't fly away until we join them.

# Flower, 2001

Near a flowershop off boulevard Raspail
a woman in a sundress bending over,
I'd guess about 49 years of age
in a particular bloom, just entering
the early autumn of her life,
a thousand-year-old smile on her face
so wide open that I actually shuddered
the same shudder I did in 1989
coming over the lip of a sand dune
and seeing a big bear below me.

## Patagonia Poem

Here in the first morning sunlight I'm trying
to locate myself not by latitude 31.535646° N,
or longitude 110.747511° W, but by the skin
of my left hand at the edge of the breakfast plate.
This hand has the skin and fingers of an animal.
The right hand forks the egg of a bird, a chicken.
The bright yellow yolk was formerly alive
in the guts of the bird waiting for the absent rooster.
Since childhood it has been a struggle
not to run away and hide in a thicket and sometimes
I did so. Now I write "Jim" with egg yolk
on the white plate in order to remember my name,
and suddenly both hands look like
an animal's who also hides in a remote thicket.
I feel my head and the skull ever so slightly
beneath the skin, a primate's skull that tells
me a thicket is a good idea for my limited
intelligence, and this hand holding a pen, a truly
foreign object I love, could with its brother hand
build a shelter in which to rest awhile and take
delight in life again, to wander in the moonlight
when earth achieves its proper shape, to rest looking
out through a tangle of branches at a daylight
world that can't see back in at this animal shape.

# Reading Calasso

I'm the pet dog of a family of gods
who never gave me any training.
Usually they are remote.
I curl up in an empty house
and they peek in the window when I'm sleeping.
Their children feed me table scraps
from ink-stained fingers.
Sometimes they lock me in a shed
and keep calling my name outside the door.
They expect me to bark day and night
because nearly everyone is their enemy.

## The Bear

When my propane ran out
when I was gone and the food
thawed in the freezer I grieved
over the five pounds of melted squid,
but then a big gaunt bear arrived
and feasted on the garbage, a few tentacles
left in the grass, purplish white worms.
O bear, now that you've tasted the ocean
I hope your dreamlife contains the whales
I've seen, that one in the Humboldt current
basking on the surface who seemed to watch
the seabirds wheeling around her head.

# Bars

Too much money-talk sucks the juice
out of my heart. Despite a fat wallet
I always become a welfare mother trying to raise
the price of a chicken for my seven children,
the future characters of my novels
who are inside me wanting to go to a bar.
They're choking on unwritten book dust and need
a few drinks as much as I do. (We're all
waiting to see what we become when we're grown up.)
Everyone smart knows that alcohol is life's
consolation prize for the permanently inconsolable.
Even my unborn characters who right now
are simpleminded demons sense the drinks
waiting for them when their bodies reach solid ground.
At four PM I resist for moments, head for the Bluebird
where in the parking lot I become a prescient animal,
probably a stray dog, hearing the ass-cheek squeak
of a woman passing on the sidewalk. A small male
fly follows her swinging left ankle and smiles
looking upward in the season of summer dresses.
One drink and I'm petulant. Men in golf clothes
are talking about the stock market where once
men talked of farming, hunting, fishing, the weather.
If Holly weren't sitting jauntily on a bar stool
I'd gulp and bolt. Something about a bar stool
that loves a woman's bottom. Vodka makes me young
but not young enough and the men keep saying Lucent
Lucent Lucent. Secret powers only allow
me two drinks before dinner so I head for Dick's Tavern
where actual working men talk of fishing,

crops, bankrupt orchards, the fact that the moon
is a bit smaller than it used to be. No one says Lucent,
only that the walleyes are biting short, but Lucent,
this preposterous French word afflicting so many
with melancholy, carries me back to Paris
where dozens of times I've entered the Select
on Montparnasse with hungry heart and mind.
When I'm there next month I'll order my bottle
of Brouilly, perhaps a herring salad, say "Lucent"
loudly to a woman to see what happens. Wine
makes me younger than vodka and while I drink
I'll pet the cat who after a dozen years will finally
sit on my lap, and think we're better at nearly
everything than the French except how to live life,
a small item indeed. Once I left the Select
for the airport, de Gaulle, and twenty-four hours
later I was sitting in my cabin in the Upper Peninsula
waiting for a sow bear and two cubs to leave
the clearing so I could go to the bar, The Dunes Saloon,
and think over France in tranquility. The idea
of going to this bar draws in creature life. Once in the driveway
a female wolf stood in my headlights and nodded,
obviously the reincarnation of a girl I knew
who drowned in Key West where I first discovered
that one drink can break the gray egg that sometimes
encloses you, two drinks help you see this world.
Three drinks and you're back inside the gray egg.

# Diabetes

I'm drawing blood the night of the full moon,
also a full eclipse of the full moon.
When will this happen again in my life,
if ever? Maybe in yours, of course.
I'm drawing blood not in Vampirism
but in diabetes. Few can find the Carpathians
on the map. It would be unhealthy for a vampire
to drink my sugary blood, which is a river
miles in length, a rare round river,
billions of round rivers walking the earth
and flowing with blood. A needle pops
the finger and out it comes, always a surprise,
red as a rose rose red my heart pumps flower red.
You wonder who created this juice of life?
And what power in the blood, as the hymn goes.
The grizzly flips the huge dead buffalo like a pancake.
The bloody brain concocts its mysteries, Kennedy's
fragments flying forever through the air in our neurons.
Walking outside with a bloody smear on my tingling
finger I stare at the half-shadowed bloodless
moon. Fifty yards away in September wolves killed
three of Bob Webber's sheep. My wife Linda called
me in Paris to say that from our bedroom window
before dawn you could hear them eating the sheep.
Red blood on the beige grass of late September.

# Searchers

At dawn Warren is on my bed,
a ragged lump of fur listening
to the birds as if deciding whether or not
to catch one. He has an old man's
mimsy delusion. A rabbit runs across
the yard and he walks after it
thinking he might close the widening distance
just as when I followed a lovely woman
on boulevard Montparnasse but couldn't equal
her rapid pace, the click-click of her shoes
moving into the distance, turning the final
corner, but when I turned the corner
she had disappeared and I looked up
into the trees thinking she might have climbed one.
When I was young a country girl would climb
a tree and throw apples down at my upturned face.
Warren and I are both searchers. He's looking
for his dead sister Shirley, and I'm wondering
about my brother John who left the earth
on this voyage all living creatures take.
Both cat and man are bathed in pleasant
insignificance, their eyes fixed on birds and stars.

# Mother Night

When you wake at three AM you don't think
of your age or sex and rarely your name
or the plot of your life which has never
broken itself down into logical pieces.
At three AM you have the gift of incomprehension
wherein the galaxies make more sense
than your job or the government. Jesus at the well
with Mary Magdalene is much more vivid
than your car. You can clearly see the bear
climb to heaven on a golden rope in the children's
story no one ever wrote. Your childhood horse
named June still stomps the ground for an apple.
What is morning and what if it doesn't arrive?
One morning Mother dropped an egg and asked
me if God was the same species as we are?
Smear of light at five AM. Sound of Webber's
sheep flock and sandhill cranes across the road,
burble of irrigation ditch beneath my window.
She said, "Only lunatics save newspapers
and magazines," fried me two eggs, then said,
"If you want to understand mortality look at birds."
Blue moon, two full moons this month,
which I conclude are two full moons. In what
direction do the dead fly off the earth?
Rising sun. A thousand blackbirds pronounce day.

# The Creek

One. Two. Three.
Before six AM waking
to the improbable ache of confused
dreams so that the open world
of consciousness was to jump into hell.
Fled the house with my dog Rose,
crossed the creek and into a thicket
after counting three different beer cans
by the road, two varieties of water bottles.
Who hears?
asked the man with ears.
Eleven different birdcalls
and a vermilion flycatcher just beyond
my nose fluttering along a willow
branch unsure of my company
during his bug breakfast.
Who hears? Far above a soundless gray hawk
attacks and chases away two turkey vultures.
Looked up again and sensed the dead
lounging upon those billowing cumulus clouds.
I'll check on this the next time I fly.

# Birds Again

A secret came a week ago though I already
knew it just beyond the bruised lips of consciousness.
The very alive souls of thirty-five hundred dead birds
are harbored in my body. It's not uncomfortable.
I'm only temporary habitat for these not-quite-
weightless creatures. I offered a wordless invitation
and now they're roosting within me, recalling
how I had watched them at night
in fall and spring passing across earth moons,
little clouds of black confetti, chattering and singing
on their way north or south. Now in my dreams
I see from the air the rumpled green and beige,
the watery face of earth as if they're carrying
me rather than me carrying them. Next winter
I'll release them near the estuary west of Alvarado
and south of Veracruz. I can see them perching
on undiscovered Olmec heads. We'll say goodbye
and I'll return my dreams to earth.

# Becoming

Nowhere is it the same place as yesterday.
None of us is the same person as yesterday.
We finally die from the exhaustion of becoming.
This downward cellular jubilance is shared
by the wind, bugs, birds, bears and rivers,
and perhaps the black holes in galactic space
where our souls will all be gathered in an invisible
thimble of antimatter. But we're getting ahead of ourselves.
Yes, trees wear out as the wattles under my chin
grow, the wrinkled hands that tried to strangle
a wife beater in New York City in 1957.
We whirl with the earth, catching our breath
as someone else, our soft brains ill-trained
except to watch ourselves disappear into the distance.
Still, we love to make music of this puzzle.

## Portal, Arizona

I've been apart too long
from this life we have.
They deep-fry pork chops locally.
I've never had them that way.
In the canyon at dawn the Cooper's hawk
rose from her nest. Lion's pug marks
a few miles up where the canyon narrowed
and one rock had an eye with sky beyond.
A geezer told me Nabokov wrote here
while his beloved Vera tortured the piano.
He chased butterflies to their pinheaded doom
but Lolita survived. What beauty
can I imagine beyond these vast rock walls
with caves sculpted by wind where perhaps
Geronimo slept quite innocent of television
and when his three-year-old son died
made a war these ravens still talk about.

# Easter Morning

On Easter morning all over America
the peasants are frying potatoes
in bacon grease.

We're not supposed to have "peasants"
but there are tens of millions of them
frying potatoes on Easter morning,
cheap and delicious with catsup.

If Jesus were here this morning he might
be eating fried potatoes with my friend
who has a '51 Dodge and a '72 Pontiac.

When his kids ask why they don't have
a new car he says, "These cars were new once
and now they are experienced."

He can fix anything and when rich folks
call to get a toilet repaired he pauses
extra hours so that they can further
learn what we're made of.

I told him that in Mexico the poor say
that when there's lightning the rich
think that God is taking their picture.
He laughed.

Like peasants everywhere in the history
of the world ours can't figure out why
they're getting poorer. Their sons join
the army to get work being shot at.

Your ideals are invisible clouds
so try not to suffocate the poor,
the peasants, with your sympathies.
They know that you're staring at them.

# Corrido Sonorense

*para la banda Los Humildes*

Cuando ella cantó su canción
aun los conejos y los perros rabiosos escucharon.
Vivía en una choza de estaño
a mitad de camino de una montaña cerca de Caborca.
Sólo tenía doce años, criada por un hermano
que algún viernes se fue a Hermosillo
para engañar a los ricos y poderosos
que le habían robado su cosecha.
Tres días y tres noches
esperaba con el corazón en la boca
al final de su sendero al borde
del camino polvoriento que conducía a Caborca.
Hacía calor y estaba tomando el aire
en sollozos cuando un camión se acercó
y le tiró un saco con la risa
de un diablo frío. En el saco
estaban la lengua de su hermano y su dedo
con el anillo hecho de crin.
Ahora se convertiría en puta o moriría de hambre,
pero se cortó las venas para reunirse con su hermano.
Si deseas engañar a los ricos y poderosos
tienes que hacerlo con un arma.

# Sonoran Corrida

*for the band Los Humildes*

When she sang her song
even rabbits and mad dogs listened.
She lived in a tin shack
halfway up a mountain near Caborca.
She was only twelve, raised by a brother
who one Friday went to Hermosillo
to cheat the rich and powerful
who had stolen his crop.
Three days and three nights
she waited with her heart in her throat
at the end of their path down
to the dusty road that led to Caborca.
It was hot and she was drinking the air
in sobs when a truck drew up
and threw her a bag with a cold
devil's laughter. In the bag
were her brother's tongue and finger
with its ring made of a horsehair nail.
Now she would become a whore or starve,
but she cut her wrists to join her brother.
If you wish to cheat the rich and powerful
you must do it with a gun.

## Older Love

His wife has asthma
so he only smokes outdoors
or late at night with head
and shoulders well into
the fireplace, the mesquite and oak
heat bright against his face.
Does it replace the heat
that has wandered from love
back into the natural world?
But then the shadow passion casts
is much longer than passion,
stretching with effort from year to year.
Outside tonight hard wind and sleet
from three bald mountains,
and on the hearth before his face
the ashes we'll all become,
soft as the back of a woman's knee.

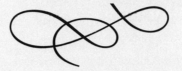

## Los viejos tiempos

En los viejos tiempos no oscurecía hasta medianoche
y la lluvia y la nieve emergían de la tierra
en vez de caer del cielo. Las mujeres eran fáciles.
Cada vez que veías una, dos más aparecían,
caminando hacia ti marcha atrás al tiempo que su ropa caía.
El dinero no crecía en las hojas de los árboles sino abrazado
a los troncos en billeteras de ternero,
pero sólo podías sacar veinte dólares al día.
Ciertos hombres volaban tan bien como los cuervos mientras
       otros trepaban
los árboles cual ardillas. A siete mujeres de Nebraska
se les tomó el tiempo nadando río arriba en el Misuri;
fueron más veloces que los delfines moteados del lugar. Los
       perros basenji
podían hablar español, mas decidieron no hacerlo.
Unos políticos fueron ejecutados por traicionar
la confianza pública y a los poetas se les dio la ración de un galón
de vino tinto al día. La gente sólo moría un día
al año y bellos coros surgían como por un embudo
a través de las chimeneas de los hospitales donde cada habitación tenía
un hogar de piedra. Algunos pescadores aprendieron a caminar
sobre el agua y de niño yo trotaba por los ríos,
mi caña de pescar siempre lista. Las mujeres que anhelaban el amor
sólo necesitaban usar pantuflas de oreja de cerdo o aretes
de ajo. Todos los perros y la gente en libre concurso
se tornaban de tamaño mediano y color marrón, y en Navidad
todos ganaban la lotería de cien dólares. Ni Dios ni Jesús
tenían que descender a la tierra porque ya estaban
aquí montando caballos salvajes cada noche
y a los niños se les permitía ir a la cama tarde para oírlos

# The Old Days

In the old days it stayed light until midnight
and rain and snow came up from the ground
rather than down from the sky. Women were easy.
Every time you'd see one, two more would appear,
walking toward you backwards as their clothes dropped.
Money didn't grow in the leaves of trees but around
the trunks in calf's leather money belts,
though you could only take twenty bucks a day.
Certain men flew as well as crows while others ran
up trees like chipmunks. Seven Nebraska women
were clocked swimming upstream in the Missouri
faster than the local spotted dolphins. Basenjis
could talk Spanish but all of them chose not to.
A few political leaders were executed for betraying
the public trust and poets were rationed a gallon
of Burgundy a day. People only died on one day
a year and lovely choruses funneled out
of hospital chimneys where every room had a field-
stone fireplace. Some fishermen learned to walk
on water and as a boy I trotted down rivers,
my flyrod at the ready. Women who wanted love
needed only to wear pig's ear slippers or garlic
earrings. All dogs and people in free concourse
became medium sized and brown, and on Christmas
everyone won the hundred-dollar lottery. God and Jesus
didn't need to come down to earth because they were
already here riding wild horses every night
and children were allowed to stay up late to hear

pasar al galope. Los mejores restaurantes eran iglesias
donde los anglicanos servían cocina provenzal, los metodistas toscana
y así. En ese tiempo el país era dos mil millas
más ancho, y mil millas más
profundo. Había muchos valles para caminar aún no descubiertos
donde tribus indígenas vivían en paz
aunque algunas tribus eligieron fundar naciones nuevas
en las áreas desconocidas hasta entonces en las negras
grietas de los límites entre los estados. Me casé
con una joven pawnee en una ceremonia detrás de la catarata
      acostumbrada.
Las cortes estaban administradas por osos durmientes y pájaros cantaban
fábulas lúcidas de sus pájaros ancestros que vuelan ahora
en otros mundos. Algunos ríos fluían demasiado rápido
para ser útiles pero se les permitió hacerlo cuando acordaron
no inundar la Conferencia de Des Moines.
Los aviones de pasajeros se parecían a barcos aéreos con múltiples
alas aleteantes que tocaban un tipo de música de salón
en el cielo. Las consólidas crecían en los cañones de pistola
y cada quien podía seleccionar siete días al año
con libertad de repetir pero este no era un programa
popular. En esos días el vacío giraba
con flores y animales salvajes desconocidos asistían
a funerales campestres. Todos los tejados en las ciudades
eran huertas de flores y verduras. El río Hudson era potable
y una ballena jorobada fue vista cerca del muelle
de la calle 42, su cabeza llena de la sangre azul del mar,
su voz alzando las pisadas de la gente
en su tradicional antimarcha, su inocuo desarreglo.
Podría seguir pero no lo haré. Toda mi evidencia
se perdió en un incendio pero no antes que fuera masticada
por todos los perros que habitan la memoria.
Uno tras otro ladran al sol, a la luna y las estrellas
tratando de acercarlas otra vez.

them galloping by. The best restaurants were churches,
with Episcopalians serving Provençal, the Methodists Tuscan,
and so on. In those days the country was an extra
two thousand miles wider, and an additional thousand
miles deep. There were many undiscovered valleys
to walk in where Indian tribes lived undisturbed
though some tribes chose to found new nations
in the heretofore unknown areas between the black
boundary cracks between states. I was married
to a Pawnee girl in a ceremony behind the usual waterfall.
Courts were manned by sleeping bears and birds sang
lucid tales of ancient bird ancestors who now fly
in other worlds. Certain rivers ran too fast
to be usable but were allowed to do so when they consented
not to flood at the Des Moines Conference.
Airliners were similar to airborne ships with multiple
fluttering wings that played a kind of chamber music
in the sky. Pistol barrels grew delphiniums
and everyone was able to select seven days a year
they were free to repeat but this wasn't a popular
program. In those days the void whirled
with flowers and unknown wild animals attended
country funerals. All the rooftops in cities were flower
and vegetable gardens. The Hudson River was drinkable
and a humpback whale was seen near the Forty-second Street
pier, its head full of the blue blood of the sea,
its voice lifting the steps of people
in their traditional anti-march, their harmless disarray.
I could go on but won't. All my evidence
was lost in a fire but not before it was chewed
on by all the dogs who inhabit memory.
One by one they bark at the sun, moon and stars
trying to draw them closer again.

# Two Girls

Late November (full moon last night),
a cold Patagonia moon, the misty air
tinkled slightly, a rank-smelling bull
in the creek bottom seemed to be crying.
Coyotes yelped up the canyon
where they took a trip-wire photo of a jaguar
last spring. I hope he's sleeping or eating
a delicious deer. Our two little girl dogs
are peeing in the midnight yard, nervous
about the bull. They can't imagine a jaguar.

# The Little Appearances of God

I

When god visits us he sleeps
without a clock in empty bird nests.
He likes the view. Not too high.
Not too low. He winks a friendly wink
at a nearby possum who sniffs the air
unable to detect the scent
of this not-quite-visible stranger.
A canyon wren lands on the bridge
of god's nose deciding the new experience
is worth the fear. He's an old bird
due to flee the earth
not on his own wings. This is a good
place to feel his waning flutter
of breath, hear his last delicate musical
call, his death song, and then he hopes
to become part of god's body. Feeling
the subdued dread of his illness
he won't know for sure until it's over.

II

He's now within the form of a whip-poor-will
sitting on a faded gravestone in the twilight
while children pass by the cemetery
almost enjoying the purity of their fright.
Since he's god he can read the gravestone
upside down. Little Mary disappeared
in the influenza epidemic back in 1919.
He ponders that it took a couple of million

years to invent these children but perhaps microbes
must also have freedom from predestination.
He's so tired of hearing about this ditzy Irishman,
Bishop Ussher, who spread the rumor that creation
only took six thousand years when it required twelve billion.
Man shrunk himself with the biological hysteria
of clocks, the machinery of dread. You spend twelve billion
years inventing ninety billion galaxies and who appreciates
your work except children, birds and dogs, and a few
other genius strokes like otters and porpoises, those humans
who kiss joy as it flies, who see though not with the eye.

III

Years ago he kept an eye on DePrise Brescia,
a creature of beauty. He doesn't lose track of people
as some need no help, bent to their own particulars.
No dancing or music allowed.
The world in front of their noses has disappeared.
Dickinson wrote, "The Brain is just the weight of God."
We said goodbye to our farm and a stately heron walked up the steps
and looked in our window. I had suffocated myself
but then south of Zihuatanejo just outside the Pacific's
crashing and lethal surf in a panga I heard the billions
of cicadas in the wild bougainvillea on the mountainsides,
a new kind of thunder. He gave Thoreau, Modigliani
and Neruda the same birthday to tease with his abilities.

# Waves

A wave lasts only moments
but underneath another one is always
waiting to be born. This isn't the Tao
of people but of waves.
As a student of people, waves, the Tao,
I'm free to let you know that waves
and people tell the same story
of how blood and water were born,
that our bodies are full of creeks
and rivers flowing in circles,
that we are kin of the waves
and the nearly undetectable ocean currents,
that the moon pleads innocence
of its tidal power, its wayward control
of our dreams, the way the moon tugs
at our skulls and loins, the way
the tides make their tortuous love to the land.
We're surely creatures with unknown gods.

# Time

Nothing quite so wrenches
the universe like time.
It clings obnoxiously
to every atom, not to speak
of the moon, which it weighs
down with invisible wet dust.
I used to think the problem
was space, the million miles
between me and the pretty waitress
across the diner counter stretching
to fill the coffee machine with water,
but now I know it's time
which withers me moment by moment
with her own galactic smile.

# An Old Man

Truly old men, he thought, don't look too far past the applesauce and cottage cheese, filling the tank of the kerosene heater over there in the corner of the cabin near the stack of *National Geographics* from the forties containing nipples from Borneo and the Amazon, tattooed and pierced. He carries extra cash because he woke up on a recent morning thinking that the ATM at the IGA had acted suspiciously. The newspaper said pork steak was ninety-nine cents a pound but it turned out to be a newspaper from last week and pork steak had shot up to one thirty-nine. He can't eat all the fish he catches and sometimes the extras get pushed toward the back of the refrigerator so that the rare visitor says, "Jesus Christ Frank something stinks." A feral tomcat that sometimes sleeps in the pump shed will eat it anyway. He read that his thin hair will continue growing in the grave, a nice idea but then cremation is cheaper. His great-granddaughter from way downstate wears an African-type nose ring and brought him a bird book but he'd rather know what birds call themselves. He often dreams of the nine dogs of his life and idly wonders if he'll see them again. He's not counting on it but it's another nice idea. One summer night in a big moon he walked three miles to his favorite bend of the river and sat on a stump until first light when a small bear swam past. In the night his ghost wife appeared and asked, "Frank, I miss you, aren't you holding on too long?" and he said, "It's not for me to decide." Last November he made a big batch of chili from a hindquarter of a bear a neighbor shot. There are seven containers left and they shouldn't go to waste. Waste not, want not.

# To a Meadowlark

*for M.L. Smoker*

Up on the Fort Peck Reservation
(Assiniboine and Sioux)
just as I passed two white crosses
in the ditch I hit a fledgling meadowlark,
the slightest thunk against the car's grille.
A mean-minded God
in a mean-minded machine, offering
another ghost to the void to join the two
white crosses stabbing upward in the insufferable
air. Wherever we go we do harm, forgiving
ourselves as wheels do cement for wearing
each other out. We set this house
on fire forgetting that we live within.

Driving south of Wolf Point down by the Missouri:
M.L. Smoker is camped with her Indians,
tepees in a circle, eating buffalo meat for breakfast,
reminding themselves what life may have been.
She says that in the evenings the wild horses
from the *terra incognita* to the south come
to the river to drink and just stand there
watching the Indians dance. I leave quickly,
still feeling like a bullsnake whipping through
the grass looking for something to kill.

# November

The souls of dogs,
big toes of ladies,
original clouds,
the winter life
of farm machinery,
the hammer lost
in the weeds,
the filaments of sunlight
hugging the bare tree,
then slipping off the bark
down into night.

## Cold Poem

A cold has put me on the fritz, said Eugene O'Neill,
how can I forget certain things?
Now I have thirteen bottles of red wine
where once I had over a thousand.
I know where they went but why should I tell?
Every day I feed the dogs and birds.
The yard is littered with bones and seed husks.
Hearts spend their entire lives in the dark,
but the dogs and birds are fond of me.
I take a shower frequently but still
women are not drawn to me in large numbers.
Perhaps they know I'm happily married
and why exhaust themselves vainly to seduce me?
I loaned hundreds of thousands of dollars
and was paid back only by two Indians.
If I had known history it was never otherwise.
This is the song of the cold when people
are themselves but less so, people
who haven't listened to my unworded advice.
I was once described as "immortal"
but this didn't include my mother who recently died.
And why go to New York after the asteroid
and the floods of polar waters, the crumbling
buildings, when you're the only one there
in 2050? Come back to earth.
Blow your nose and dwell on the shortness of life.
Lift up your dark heart and sing a song about
how time drifts past you like the gentlest, almost
imperceptible breeze.

# Invasive

Coming out of anesthesia I believed
I had awakened in the wrong body,
and when I returned to my snazzy hotel room
and looked at *Architectural Digest*
I no longer recognized large parts of the world.
There was a cabin for sale
for seven million dollars, while mine had cost
only forty grand with forty acres. An android
from drugs I understood finally that life
works to no one's advantage. From dawn
until midnight I put together a jigsaw puzzle
made of ten million pieces of white confetti.
On television I watch the overburdened world
of books and movies, all flickering trash, while outside
cars pass through deep puddles on the street,
the swish and swash of life, patterns of rain
drizzle on the windows, finch yodel and Mexican raven squawk
until I enter the murder of sleep and fresh demons,
one of whom sings in basso profundo Mickey and Sylvia's
"Love Is Strange." In the bathroom mirror it's someone else.

# On the Way to the Doctor's

On Thursday morning at seven AM seven surgeons will spend seven
hours taking me apart and putting me back together the same way.
Three of the surgeons don't have medical degrees but are part-time
amateurs trying to learn the ropes. One is a butcher who wants to
move up. A butcher's salary is twenty-seven thousand and the aver-
age surgeon makes two hundred twenty-seven, the difference being
the proximity of the nearest huge asteroid to the moon, which could
be destroyed any minute now. In anticipation of the unmentionable
I've put my life in order. Anyone with blood-slippery hands can drop
a heart on the floor. I've sent a single-page letter of resignation to the
Literary World but they haven't had time to read it. They're exhausted
from reading Sontag's obituaries, a nasty reminder that everyone dies.
Assuming I survive, Jean Peters and Jean Simmons will reemerge as
twenty-seven-year-olds and trade shifts nursing me around the clock.
They're goddesses and never get tired. Since the surgeons are cutting
me open like a baked potato, sex will be put aside for the time being.
It's unpleasant to burst your stitches on a Sunday morning dalliance
when you're due on your gurney in the hospital Chapel of Black
Roses. I'm not afraid of death. I've been told I'll immediately return
as a common house finch, but it's all the stuff between here and death
falsely called life. Right now we're actually in the car with my wife
driving to the doctor's. I say, "Turn left on Ruthrauff onto La Cholla."
I always drive when we go to Tucson but I'm in too much pain half-
reclining in the seat peeking out like the little old man I might not
get to be. At the entrance to the office the doctor meets us with an
immense bouquet of Brazilian tropical flowers. The doctor resembles
a photo of my mother in 1933, so much so that I'm uncomfortable.
The office is full of dozens of identical framed photos of a desperate
sunset in the desert trying to look original. The office temperature is
kept at 32 degrees to reduce odors. I've been recently sleeping under

seven blankets and am quite cold. The pages of the magazines on the coffee table are blank so that you can make up your own *National Geographics*. I haven't eaten for days except rice and yogurt, but my wife is out in the car having a baguette stuffed with proscuitto, imported provolone, mortadella and roasted peppers. They turn out the lights so my eyes don't tire reading blank pages. Now I see that the mirror on the wall is two-way and in another room the seven surgeons are rolling up their sleeves, hot to get started. "We don't have time to wash our hands," they say in unison.

## Español

Por años he creído que el mundo debe hablar español.
He soñado que hablaba y leía español,
pero cuando desperté no fue verdad. Tal vez las Naciones Unidas
puedan poner freno al inglés pero lo dudo.
El inglés es el lenguaje de la conquista, el dinero, el asesinato.

Dios me envió un e-mail diciendo que el sexo sería mejor
en español. Dios estaba fumando un "Lucky Strike"
mientras Bush mordisqueaba chicle "Dentyne" y estudiaba "Baywatch"
      en la tele.

Mi viejo amigo Jesús se convirtió en una película de terror
que ganó millones en inglés, el cual pensaba no había sido inventado.
Jesús habla español pero no entiende bien el inglés,
por eso nuestras oraciones erran y las chicas son deshimenizadas.

Niños y niñas yacen en sus camas pataleando
en desesperación a los dioses que juegan al boliche
con sus cabezas. No pasaría si hablaran español.
La televisión mexicana dijo que la Virgen llevaba calzones los domingos.

El dibujo animado es nuestra forma de arte mientras que los españoles
      escriben
poesía, miles de Lorcas de quinta elogiando a la luna
pero sin el contragiro de los dibujos en sus corazones. El sexo no
      nos conducirá
al cielo en español pero nos acercará más que los dibujos.

María Magdalena dijo que si no hubiera sido por la historia
se habría ahogado en el pozo o inventado

# Spanish

For years I've believed the world should speak Spanish.
I've dreamt that I spoke and read Spanish,
but when I awoke it wasn't true. Perhaps the U.N.
can put a halt to English but I doubt it.
English is the language of conquest, money, murder.

God e-mailed me that sex would be better
in Spanish. God was smoking a Lucky Strike
while Bush snapped Dentyne and studied *Baywatch* on TV.

My old pal Jesus became a horror film that made
millions in English that he thought hadn't been invented.
Jesus speaks Spanish but understands English poorly,
thus our prayers go awry and girls are dehymenized.

Boys and girls lie on their beds kicking their feet
in desperation at the gods who are bowling
with their heads. It wouldn't happen if they spoke Spanish.
Mexican TV said the Virgin wore underpants on Sunday.

The cartoon is our art form while the Spanish write
poetry, thousands of fifth-rate Lorcas praising the moon
but without cartoon backspin in their hearts. Sex won't take
us to heaven in Spanish but closer than cartoons.

Mary Magdalene said that if it hadn't been for history
she would have drowned herself at the well or invented

la pistola para que se la dispararan. Es tan compleja
que no puede ser entendida excepto en español.

Me arrojé de un avión pero aterricé en una nube de español.
El inglés me había perseguido a muerte. Los santos caen
sobre plumas ensangrentadas justo antes que la historia termine.

the gun for them to shoot her. She's so complex
that she can't be understood except in Spanish.

I jumped out of a plane but landed on a Spanish cloud.
English had chased me to death. The saints fall
on bloody feathers just before history ends.

## Pico

I don't know what. I don't know what.
I'm modern man at the crossroads,
an interstice where ten thousand roads meet
and exfoliate. Meanwhile today a hundred
dense blue never-seen-before pinyon jays
land in the yard for a scant ten minutes.
The pinyon jays are not at any crossroads
but are finding their way south by celestial navigation.
You're not on a road, you fool. This life
is pathless with ninety billion galaxies
hovering around us, our home truly away from home.

# The Short Course

For my new part I'm in makeup
     each day for twenty-four hours.
We can die from this exhaustion
     of shooting without a script;
the lines that didn't come right disappeared
     into the thickest air
     without the vacuum of intentions.
New lines appeared in miraculous succession.
We found love by writing it down
     only moments before she appeared.
The door opened itself.
Steps were taken.
A new day dawned crimson.
We went outside among the inhuman trees.
A creek appeared from nowhere.
Everyone is raised by the gods
but we never learned our lines.

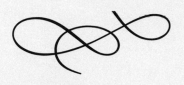

# Science

It was one of those mornings utterly distorted by the night's dreams. Why go to court to change my name to Gaspar de la Nuit in order to avoid thinking of myself as a silly, fat old man? At midmorning I looked at the dogs as possibilities for something different in my life. I was dogsitting both daughters' dogs plus our own: Lily, Grace, Pearl, Harry, Rose and Mary. I shook the biscuit box and they assembled in the living room on a very cold windy morning when no one wanted to go outside except for a quick pee and a bark at the mailman. I sang, "He's got the whole world in his hands," as they waited for their snack. Harry was embarrassed and furtive and tried to leave the room but I called him back. I tried, "Yes, we have no bananas, we have no bananas today," and Lily, the largest of the dogs, became angry at the others who looked away intimidated. I tried something religious, "The Old Rugged Cross," to no particular response except that Mary leapt up at the biscuit box in irritation. I realized decisively that dogs don't care about music and religion and thus have written up this report. This scarcely makes me the Father of the A-bomb, I thought as I flung the contents of the full box of biscuits around the room with the dogs scrambling wildly on the hard maple floor. Let there be happy chaos.

# The Fish in My Life

When I was younger I walked the floor
of the Baltic looking for a perfect herring.

Off Ecuador when I swam underneath the boat
the hooked marlin was wreathed in curious sea snakes.

I stepped on a scorpion in Key West. It bit me.
It's not a fish but it looks like a shrimp.

The nude girl ate the brook trout I fried. A morsel
plummeted from her lips to the left aureole.

Fish spend their lives underwater except for skyward jumps
for food, or to shake off gill lice, look around in dismay.

In the house of water the bottom and the top
do not go away. Our drowned bodies are kissed.

With my grandson's Play-Doh I shaped
a modest fish, also the brown girl of my dreams.

O fish, my brothers and sisters, some scientists
think that our sinuses are merely vestigial gills.

Fish, we both survive among countless thousands
of dead eggs. We're well chosen by the gods of chaos.

# A Letter to Ted & Dan

*France to Michigan*


Just another plane trip
with the mind wandering
at large in the bowels
of life. How am I to land this?
At Godthåb, above Greenland,
we're disappointing compared to the immensity
of our scientific reality, the trillions
of unresolved particles, though there were
those improbable unrecorded celebrations,
over a million at the samba festival,
a thousand bands, a million doves
eaten raw because there was no wood for fire,
an immense dance with no words with nonstop
loving in the fashion of lions and porpoises.
Off in the jungle anacondas perked up their heads
and slowly moved toward the music,
the largest snake of all wrapped around
the world's waist, holding us together
against our various defilements, our naive
theocracies at war with one another.


                    •—•


Almost forgot that, over Iceland,
seven miles below I saw children
sledding in the first snow of the year,
small as motes of dust on silver-edged
sleighs, the glistening of the frosted sweat
of the shaggy pony that pulled them

back up the hill. I've long wondered
at the way certain children, even babies,
decide to become songbirds because they could see
the endless suffering in their future.
They've been using this method for centuries.

•◆•

I've asked the French government,
Richelieu in fact, for the use of a one-room
cabin in the Dordogne where I can recreate
the local origin of man in this birthplace
of the Occident, riding the spear
of the Occident into the future, the iron horse
that makes us glue the life of mankind
together with blood.

•◆•

In France I went to a place
of grandeur though it was only
a thicket as large as the average hotel room.
I learned that we'll float into eternity
like the dehydrated maggots I saw
in Mexico around the body of a desert tortoise
missing an interior that had fled
seven days before. How grand.

•◆•

For after death I've been given
the false biblical promise of smoking privileges
and the possession of hundreds of small
photos of all the dogs and women I've known.

The beasts (the plane and I) land on earth.
Time for a hot dog and a small pizza.
I glance at the mellifluous rubbing
of a melancholy woman's buttocks.
I tell her to celebrate her tears.

# Effluvia

Tonight the newish moon is orange
from the smoke of a forest fire, a wedge of fresh orange.

The mystery of ink pumped up from three
thousand feet in northern Michigan from the bed
of a Pleistocene sea. A meteor hit
a massive group of giant squid, some say
millions, from whose ink I write this poem.

A bold girl I once knew made love
on lysergic acid to a dolphin and a chimp,
though not the same day. She said the chimp
was too hairy, too fast, and improbably insensitive.

An artist friend made me a cocktail shaker
from a rubbery translucent material and in the pinkish
form of a human stomach. Shake it and the vodka
drops like rain into a sea of happiness.

I am a relic in a reliquary.
All of these damp skulls of ghosts,
many of them feathered, telling
me that the past isn't very past.

On an airliner going to both dream coasts
I'm a Romantic Poet so alone and lonely.
Lucky for me there are pilots up front.

We must give our fantasy women homely names
to keep our feet barely on the ground of this dismembered

earth: Wilma, Edna, Ethel, Blanche, Frida.
Otherwise we'll fly away on the backs
of their somnambulistic lust, fleas in their plumage.

The birds above the river yesterday: Swainson's
hawk, prairie and peregrine falcons, bald and golden
eagles, osprey, wild geese, fifty-two sandhill cranes.
Their soaring bodies nearly lifting us from the river.

# Joseph's Poem

It's the date that gets me
down. It keeps changing.
Others have noticed this.
Not long ago up at Hard Luck Ranch,
Diana, the cow dog, was young.
Now her face looks like my own.
Surprise, she doesn't say, with each
halting step, the world is going away.
How could I have thought otherwise,
these dogging steps pit-patting
to and fro, though when the soul
rises to the moment, moment by moment
it is otherwise. Dog's foot is holy
and the geezer, childish again,
is deep up a canyon with his dog
close to the edge of the world,
the heart beating a thousand times
a minute, probably more,
as if it were an interior propeller
to whir us upward, but it's not.
Once I held the heart of a bear
that was about my size. Stewed it back
at the cabin and thought that the sky
opened up and changed her colors,
smelled the fumes of a falling contrail,
sensed the world behind my back
and beneath my feet, ravens above,
each tree its individual odor,
the night no longer night,
the burst of water around my body,
the world unfolding in glory with each step.

# Unbuilding

It's harder
to dismantle your life
than build it.
One Sunday morning at Hard Luck Ranch
the roadrunner flits around the backyard
like an American poet,
ignored by nine cow dogs lying in patches
of sun, also by three ravens,
and finally by seven Gambel's quail
who do not know that they're delicious roasted
when they come to the bowl of water.
It is always possible to see the traceries of birds,
but on the scrambled porn channel the woman's
mouth that prays is used otherwise and the ground
delivers up insects I've never noticed before.
I found myself in the slightest prayer
for Diana who I fear will die like her
namesake did far across the ocean blue.
She's fourteen with cancer of the mouth
and throat though around Christmastime
I found her making love with her son Ace.
When they finished I gave her extra biscuits
for being so human, for staying as young
as her mind and body called out for her to be.
No rain now for one hundred twenty-three days
so I read Su Tung-p'o where it's always raining,
*Rain drenches down as from a tilted basin,*
and recall I owe forty thousand on my credit cards.
Carried along by red wine and birds, dogs,
the roadrunner's charm, I take apart my life
stone by mortared stone while I'm still strong

enough to do so, or think that I am,
wishing that I could smile like a lazy
dog curled in the dust on Sunday morning,
far from the shroud I sewed for my life.

# Suzanne Wilson

Is it better to rake all the leaves
in one's life into a pile
or leave them scattered? That's a good question
as questions go, but then they're easier to burn
in one place. The years take their toll,
our lives, to be exact. We burn without fire
and without effort so slowly the wick of this lamp
seems endless. And then the fire is out,
a hallowed time. And those who took the light
with them pull us slowly toward their breasts.

## Current Events

I'm a brownish American who wonders
if civilization can be glued together with blood.
The written word is no longer understood.
We've had dogs longer than governments.
Millions of us must travel to Washington
and not talk but bark like dogs.
We must practice our barking and in unison
raise a mighty bark. The sun turns amber
and they're opening the well-oiled gates of hell.

## Poem of War (I)

The old rancher of seventy-nine years
said while branding and nutting young bulls
with the rank odor of burned hairs and flesh
in the air, the oil-slippery red nuts
plopping into a galvanized bucket,
"This smells just like Guadalcanal."

## Poem of War (II)

The theocratic cowboy forgetting Vietnam rides
into town on a red horse. He's praying to himself
not God. War prayers. The red horse
he rides is the horse of blasphemy. Jesus
leads a flower-laden donkey across the Red Sea
in the other direction, his nose full of the stink
of corpses. Buddha and Muhammad offer
cool water from a palm's shade while young
men die in the rockets' red glare.
And in the old men's dreams
René Char asked, "Who stands on the gangplank
directing operations, the captain or the rats?"
Whitman said, "So many young throats
choked on their own blood." God says nothing.

# Rachel's Bulldozer

The man sitting on the cold stone hearth
    of the fireplace
considers tomorrow, the virulent
    skirmishes with reality
he takes part in, always surprised,
    in order to earn a living.
On most days it's this villain
    reality making the heart ache,
creeping under the long shirtsleeves
    to suffocate the armpits,
each day's terror pouring vinegar
    into the heart valve.
Today it's Rachel Corrie making me
    ashamed to be human,
beating her girlish fists against
    the oncoming bulldozer blade.
Strangled mute before the television screen
    we do not deserve to witness this courage.

## After the War

God wears orange and black
on Halloween. The bumblebee hummingbird
in Cuba weighs less than a penny.

I was joined by the head to this world.
No surgery was possible.
We keep doing things together.

There's almost never a stoplight
where rivers cross each other.

Congress is as fake as television sex.
The parts are off a few inches and don't actually
meet. It's in bad taste to send the heads
of children to Washington.

Just today I noticed that all truly valuable
knowledge is lost between generations. Of course
life is upsetting. What else could be upsetting?

From not very far in space I see the tiny pink
splotches of literature here and there upon
the earth about the size of dog pounds.

Reporters mostly reported themselves.
This was a new touch. They received
producer credits and director's perks.

Tonight I smell a different kind
of darkness. The burning celluloid of news.

The Virgin strolls through Washington, D.C.,
with an ice pick shoved in her ear.

Who is taking this time machine
from the present into the present?

One of the oldest stories: dead dicks playing
with death toys. Plato said war is always greed.
Red blood turns brown in the heat. It's only
the liquid shit of slaves.

*Un mundo raro.* The angel is decidedly female.
She weighs her weight in flowers.
She has no talent for our discourse,
which she said was a septic tank burble.

Of the 90 billion galaxies a few are bad
apples, especially a fusion of male stars
not unlike galactic gay sex. Washington
is concerned, and the pope is stressed.

All over America people appear to be drinking
small bottles of water. Fill them with French
red wine and shoot out the streetlights.

As a long-lived interior astronaut
it was mostly just space. The void
was my home in which I invented
the undescribed earth.

This is Rome. There are no Christians
so we throw Muslims to the lions of war.
We have the world in the dentist's chair.

I pray daily for seven mortally ill women,
not to say that life is a mortal illness.
It's always been a matter of timing.
Lives are as hard to track as flying birds.

To understand the news is to drag a dead dog
behind you with a paper leash.
Once you loved the dog.

Try to remember all of the birds
you've heard but didn't see.
This is called grace.

I was living far too high in my mind
and started fishing like the autistic child
they found the next morning still fishing.
The war became X-rated. No American bodies.

During these times many of us
would have been far happier as fish, making
occasional little jumps up above the water's
surface for a view of the new century.

It seems that everything is a matter
of time, from cooking to dropping dead.
Just moments earlier the dead soldier
drank warm orange juice, scratched his ass
and thought about the Chicago Cubs.

Mrs. America is smothering the world
in her new pair of enormous fake tits.
She's the purgatorial mother
who can't stop eating children.

Rose was struck twice by a rattler
in the yard, a fang broken off in her eyeball.
Now old dog and old master each
have an eye full of bloody milk.

The end of the war was announced
by the Leader in a uniform from the deck
of an aircraft carrier, one of those deluxe
cruise ships that never actually touches
the lands they visit.

A girl of a different color kissed me once.
I think it was in Brazil. Celestial buttocks.
Honeysuckle dawn. Imanja rose from the sea,
her head buried in a red sun.

Hot August night, a forty-day heat wave.
Thousands of the tiniest bugs possible
are dying in this old ranch house. Like humans
they are easily attracted to the wrong light.

Tonight the moon is an orange ceiling globe
from a forest fire across the river. In the dark
animals run, stumble, run, stumble.

I stopped three feet from the top
of Everest. Fuck it, I'm not going
a single inch farther.

We need a poetry of fishscales, coxcombs,
soot, dried moss, the heated aortas of whales,
to respond to the vulpine sniggers of the gods.

Throughout history soldiers want to go to war
and when they get there straightaway wish
to go home.

Change the lens on this vast picture show.
See the mosquito's slender beak penetrate
the baby's ass. A touch of evil.

I read the unshakable dreams of the hundred-
year-old lesbian, life shorn of the perfection
of the pork chop. Everyone lacks inevitability.

Michael and Joseph never truly returned
home because they weren't the same people
they were when they left home.

My dog Rose can't stop chasing curlews
who lead her a mile this way and that.
I have to catch her before she dies of exhaustion.
This is a metaphor of nothing but itself.

The motives were somewhat imaginary but people
died in earnest. Some were
shoveled up like flattened roadkill.

During World War II my brother John
and I would holler "bombs over Tokyo"
when we pooped. A different kind of war.

She kicked her red sandal at the sun
but it landed in a parking-lot mud puddle.
"We're de-haired chimps," she said
finishing her pistachio ice-cream cone.

Osama won really big I heard on a game
show. We changed our institutions,
the surge toward a fascist Disneyland.

I wish I had danced more, said the old man
drawing nearer his death bedstead in a foot
of grass in the back forty. Where's my teddy bear?

Of late, on television we are threatened
by crocodiles, snakes and bears
in full frontal nudity. Politicians are clothed.

My childhood Jesus has become an oil guy
but then he's from the area. Seek and ye shall
find an oil well. The daughter of murder is murder.

Nothing can be understood clearly. A second into
death we'll ask, "What's happening?" Viola said
that there's an invisible world out there and we're
living within it. Rose dreams of ghost snakes.

Of late, politicians remind me of teen prostitutes
the way they sell their asses cheap, the swagger
and confusion, the girlish resolutions. They can't go
home because everyone there is embarrassed.

I nearly collapsed yesterday but couldn't find
an appropriate place. Our pieces are anchored
a thousand miles deep in molten rock. A spider-
web draws us an equal distance toward the heavens.

The Leader is confident that Jesus and the Apostles
are his invisible SWAT team. His God
is a chatterbox full of martial instructions.

I worry about the soul life of these thousand
tiny bugs that die on the midnight coffee
table. Here today, gone tomorrow, but then
in cosmic time we live a single second.

Once a year all world leaders should be put
in an Olympic swimming pool full of rotten
human blood to let them dog-paddle in their creation.
The lifeguard is a blind child playing a video war game.

Men look at women's tits and flip out.
This is the mystery of life, but then they have a line
of coke, some meth, a few beers, and beat up or rape
or shoot someone. They make movies about this.

We must adore our fatal savagery. The child
thrown naked into the snowbank for peeing the bed
then kills the neighbor's cat, etc., etc. The midget
dreamt he grew two feet. Between the Virgin
and the garrison the flower becomes a knife.

My, how our government strains us
through its filthy sheets. We're drawn
from birth through the sucking vortex
of greed. It all looked good on paper.

To change Rhys, God is a doormat in a world
full of hobnailed boots. Proud of his feet
the Leader is common change. He's everywhere.

I've been looking closely at my smaller
mythologies the better to love them, those colorful
fibs and false conclusions, the mire
of private galaxies that kept
ancient man on earth and me alive.

# Brothers and Sisters

I'm trying to open a window in this very old house of indeterminate age buried toward the back of a large ranch here in the Southwest, abandoned for so long that there's no road leading into it but a slight indentation in the pastureland, last lived in by the owner's great-uncle who moved to New York City to listen to music, or so he said, but his grandnephew said that the man was "light in his loafers," which was hard to be back in New Mexico in those days. In the pantry under a stained vinegar cruet is a sepia photo of him and his sister in their early teens on the front porch of the house, dressed unconvincingly as vaqueros, as handsome as young people get. The photo is dated 1927 and lights up the pantry. I find out that the girl died in childbirth in the middle thirties in Pasadena, the boy committed suicide in Havana in 1952, both dying in the hands of love. Out in the yard I shine my flashlight down a hole under a massive juniper stump. A rattlesnake forms itself into anxious coils surrounding its pretty babies stunned by the light.

# Fence Line Tree

There's a single tree at the fence line
here in Montana, a little like a tree
in the Sandhills of Nebraska, which may be miles
away. When I cross the unfertile pasture strewn
with rocks and the holes of gophers, badgers, coyotes,
and the rattlesnake den (a thousand killed
in a decade because they don't mix well with dogs
and children) in an hour's walking and reach
the tree, I find it oppressive. Likely it's
as old as I am, withstanding its isolation,
all gnarled and twisted from its battle
with weather. I sit against it until we merge,
and when I return home in the cold, windy
twilight I feel I've been gone for years.

# Saving Daylight

I finally got back the hour
stolen from me last spring.
What did they do with it
but put it in some nasty cold storage?
Up north a farm neighbor wouldn't change
his clocks, saying, "I'm sticking with God's time."
All of these people of late seem to know
God rather personally. God even tells
girls to limit themselves to heavy petting
and avoid the act they call "full penetration."
I don't seem to receive these instructions
that tell me to go to war, and not to look
at a married woman's butt when she leans
over to fetch a package from her car's
backseat. I'm enrolled in a school without
visible teachers, the divine mumbling
just out of earshot, the whispering from the four-million-
mile-an-hour winds on the sun. The dead rabbit
in the road spoke to me yesterday, also the owl's wing
in the garage likely torn off by a goshawk.
In this bin of ice you must carefully
try to pick the right cube.

# Incomprehension

We have running water in our
home though none of us know
why dogs exist.

Nevertheless, we love both water
and dogs and believe God might
fix our lives with his golden wrench.

This is the day the moon is closest
to us, the new moon slender
as a gray hair I pulled from my head.

The man said that there is no actual
life, only what we remember. In the
tropics the lizard is the God of the rock
he lives upon and under.

We didn't know the pages were
stuck together and we'd never
understand anything.

The church says God is a spy
who keeps track of how we misuse
our genitals. He always yawns
at the beginning of work.

I can only offer you the ten numbers
I wrote down when I read the
thermometer today, this incredible
machine I worship but don't understand.

I was the only one to see the boat sunken
on land. There were no survivors except
the few human rats that leapt like
flying squirrels.

The Queen of Earth is thought to be
up for grabs. She makes us shiver
in fear to keep us warm.

# Memorial Day

Things I didn't know about until today:
Clip your toenails when wet and they won't crack.
The white in birdfeathers comes from the moon,
the yellow from the sun,
the black from night herself.
And that at three PM today
when we have our full minute of silence
for our millions of war dead,
their ghosts beyond the invisible carapace
above the green and blue turning earth
(from which birds get other colors),
the ghosts will vomit up the remnants
of their bone dust on hearing the strident
martial music rising up to them,
the hard-peckered music of the living,
the music of the machineries of war
in the wallets of the rich. And the ghosts ask us
to send up the music of earth:
three tree frogs, two loons, splash of fish
jumping, the wind's verbless carols.

# Letter Poem to Sam Hamill and Dan Gerber

I've been translating the language with which creatures
address God, including the nonharmonic bleats
of dying sheep, the burpish fish, the tenor groan
of the toad in the snake's mouth, the croak
of the seagull flopping on the yellow line,
misnamed mockingbird and catbird singing hundreds
of borrowed songs, coyotes' joyous yipe when they
bring down a fawn that honks like a bicycle
horn for his helpless mother. The ladybug on the table
was finally still. I strained my ear close to her
during the final moments but only heard Mozart
from the other room. She was beyond reach.
One night under a big moon I heard the massive-
lunged scream of a horse pounding in the pasture
across the creek, then his breathing above the creek
gurgle. This language is closer to what we spoke
in Africa seventy thousand years ago before
we started writing things down and now we can't
seem to stop. I can't imagine how we thought that
we're better than any other creatures except that
we wrote ourselves into it. Someone looked down
from Babel's tower and got the wrong idea, ignoring
the birds above him. I learned all this one day
listening to a raven funeral in a fir tree behind
my cabin, and learned it again listening to a wolf
howling from the river delta nearby. It's an old
secret past anyone's caring, or so it seems.

Yrs,

Jim Harrison
June 20, 2001

# Hakuin and Welch

Driving with implacable Hakuin, the cruelest
teacher who ever lived, across the reaches
of Snoqualmie Pass, snow and ice after moving
upward through dense rain. The sky cleared
for a moment and did I see ornate space vehicles
against the mountain wall? I'm frankly scared
but Hakuin steadies me, not Mom who said
shame on you, or Dad so long dead his spirit
only returns to me when I'm fishing. At Jim Welch's
memorial in Seattle I could again see all human
beings and creatures flowering and dying in the void,
which is all that we are given along with the suffering
so ignored by angels. In Butte I picked up a bum
on crutches, a leg jellied in Vietnam, who took seven
prescriptions drawn from his pocket with a bottle
of pop. "Time isn't on our side," he said with the air
of a comic. I either drove through the mountains
or the mountains moved past me, the valley
rivers often flowing the wrong way. This is God's
nude world. Home, I watched the unclothed moon
rise while holding our new unruly pup
who speaks the language of Hakuin.
Protect your family. You don't know much.
Don't offer yourself up to this world.
A sense of destiny is a terrible thing.

# L'envoi

All of my life I've held myself
at an undisclosed location.
Sometimes I have a roof over my head
but no floor, and sometimes a floor but no roof.
This is the song of a man who wrote songs
without music, dog songs, river songs,
bear songs, bird songs though they didn't
need my help, and many people songs.
The just-waking universe returned the favor
with spherical carols as if creation
hadn't stopped a minute, which it hadn't,
as if our songs helped it become itself.
We gave no voice to the bear but watched
our minds allow the bear to become a bear.
At a brief still point on the whirling earth
we saw both the stars and the ground we walked
upon, struggling to recognize each other at noon,
talked ourselves deaf and blind on the sharp
edge of disappearing for reasons we never
figured out. I was conceived near a dance hall
on a bend of a river, now sixty-seven years
downstream I'm singing a water song
not struggling against the ungentle current.

# Marching

At dawn I heard among birdcalls
the billions of marching feet in the churn
and squeak of gravel, even tiny feet
still wet from the mother's amniotic fluid,
and very old halting feet, the feet
of the very light and very heavy, all marching
but not together, crisscrossing at every angle
with sincere attempts not to touch, not to bump
into each other, walking in the doors of houses
and out the back door forty years later, finally
knowing that time collapses on a single
plateau where they were all their lives,
knowing that time stops when the heart stops
as they walk off the earth into the night air.

## About the Author

Jim Harrison is a poet and novelist dividing his year between Montana and the Mexican border.

The Chinese character for poetry is made up of two parts: "word" and "temple." It also serves as pressmark for Copper Canyon Press. Founded in 1972, Copper Canyon Press remains dedicated to publishing poetry exclusively, from Nobel laureates to new and emerging authors. The Press thrives with the generous patronage of readers, writers, booksellers, librarians, teachers, students, and funders— everyone who shares the conviction that poetry invigorates the language and sharpens our appreciation of the world.

*Major funding has been provided by:*

Anonymous (2)

The Paul G. Allen Family Foundation

Lannan Foundation

National Endowment for the Arts

Washington State Arts Commission

*Copper Canyon Press gratefully acknowledges the following individuals for their generous support of this publication:*

Anonymous

Laura Chester

Bruce S. Kahn and Karen G. Hufnagle

Gregg Orr

Peter Phinny

*For information and catalogs:*

COPPER CANYON PRESS
Post Office Box 271
Port Townsend, Washington 98368
360-385-4925
www.coppercanyonpress.org

•◆•

This book is set in Dante, a font that echoes the fifteenth-century type of
Francesco Griffo. Dante was designed in 1954 by Giovanni Mardersteig. Over the
years it has been reworked by Monotype for machine and digital composition.
Book design and composition by Valerie Brewster, Scribe Typography. Printed
on archival-quality Glatfelter Author's Text at McNaughton & Gunn.

*Saving Daylight* is also issued in a signed, limited edition of 250 numbered
copies and twenty-six lettered copies, handbound by Watermark Bindery in
Port Townsend, Washington.